From the Pole to the Pulpit

Acknowledgements

Giving honor to God, who is the head of my life, the author and finisher of my faith, for without Him I am nothing. My life will forever give God praise and glory.

I want to thank Him for helping me see myself, and work through me to help others. I also want to thank myself. I feel great today, as I have come from dark places that could have prevented me from going further and seeing the great world I see today. I thank myself for recognizing the pains, having the courage to deal with them, and having the activation of wisdom to learn from them and stand strong today. Today I give thanks to my Lord and Savior, Jesus Christ.

I want to thank my beautiful daughter who has always believed in me despite all we have been through together. I want to thank those that God sent, the staff members and counselors at Mecca. I also want to thank those who took time to plant seeds in my life and water them and all of those who poured into my life and loved me unconditionally.

Dedication

This book is dedicated to my daughter, my hero and true cheerleader, Chelcie Scott, who is truly my inspiration, my joy, my everything.

I want to thank her for believing in me despite all we have been through together. Standing with me through my addiction and shortcomings, but for always believing in me, that I could make it through those dark days and very tough obstacles of life that where seen and unseen. You have help me become a better mother, person and friend. I Love you daughter.

Forward: From the Pole to the Pulpit

Words make the world go around. The human species thrives on words, like no other species known to man. Words are valuable and we need them to convey our stories. This book brings me to study two words. As I read JoAnna's story, I couldn't help but grab a plethora of valuable lessons that I can carry along my own journey in this thing called "life."

I make a conscious effort to learn from everyone I encounter, and every situation, and reading her story fulfilled the purpose of enlightenment, but most importantly, empowerment.

Empowerment is one word I think of when I read this testimony, word for word. If we are paying close attention, the feeling of empowerment can be engaged from so many directions and angles. As I read the beginning of the book, I felt her combative energy in her earlier years. The early years of life are challenging. The earlier years is when we try to understand ourselves, but we are preoccupied with learning the ways of the world and our surroundings. We are consumed with learning processes and procedures that are passed down from our elders, which takes a lot of energy. We take on ideas and opinions of others rather quickly, as we learn from watching and observing. A lot of us also take on guilt, insecurities, resentments and traumas that aren't of our own, but we get them, right? We are blindly instilled with a whole bunch of baggage that is handed down to us from our environment. If we aren't paying attention to keeping our personal growth at the forefront, it is so easy to lose ourselves with the thoughts of others, especially losing with the negative thoughts of ourselves. We learn to mask our feelings and "fit in" because what the next man in the group thinks matters to us. We want to be liked. In these chapters ahead, I learned JoAnna didn't feel liked by many people. In her mind, her self esteem was not nurtured by her surroundings. As I kept reading, it grew more and more apparent that our inward look at ourselves creates our world. Either we have a healthy, positive outlook when we see ourselves, or we don't. There is little room for meeting in the middle, because there is no middle. Our judgement of ourselves swings to the far left or the far right of the pendulum. The far good or the far bad. Our actions show us how we feel about ourselves. Our thoughts either empower the good in and around us, or our thoughts empower the bad (self-hatred, self- doubt, etc) in and around us.

I continued to read more and grew intrigued by JoAnna's inner strength. As she gets older, the trials and tribulations she is faced with can break someone to the point of no return. However, this book paints the picture of an evident God who is working, and JoAnna learning to grasp the changes He presents.

The second word that comes to mind is triumph. Triumph is an incredible feeling, and I felt this a few times in this book. The euphoria one feels from crushing a goal, fighting an obstacle and winning, going the extra mile, or simply putting one foot in front of the other intentionally, has so many rewards. I am so proud of JoAnna Davis because of the story she survived through. The ability to think through hard times doesn't come easy, and a lot of us don't make it through hard times. However, watching Mrs. Davis standing tall through all her moments is empowering for me, and I'm sure empowering for others. Triumph comes in all shapes and sizes, but the one that really leaves great impact is the triumph of defeating your lower self. When you can defeat the version of you that is against you? The version of you that is in your own way? The version of you that isn't paying attention to the higher power, and full of self-doubt and turmoil? When that version is defeated, you win and we all win. Thank you, Joanna Davis, for changing your route, being fed up, and taking your power back. Thank you for providing an example of hope and consistent, intentional work from the heart. Thank you for unleashing the power from within. With God's help, who can stop us?

- John Martin Sr.

Table of Contents

Preface

Turbulence... Turmoil... Disturbance... Chaos... Conflict. These words describe peace being broken. Abnormalities and discomfort are bred by tragic moments in early years of life. My life was never easy. This transit of life has been filled with turbulence and conflict. I'm writing the following to tell my story of pain turned to power. I'm writing to tell my story of turbulence and destruction of self, only to live to see the day where I am eager and optimistic in looking forward. Today, I am loving and anxiously waiting to see what is next for me. The difference for me in the future will be that this time around, I'm going to be at peace, have serenity, sobriety and God will be first in all actions. The art of resilience made me strong and powerful in my own life. And God gets all the Glory! Peter 3:18 But grow in the grace and knowledge of our Lord and Savior Jesus Christ. To Him be the glory both now and to the day of eternity. Amen.

Before I dive into my story, I want to thank some great people in my life. First, I want to thank God for blessing me with life after years of being mentally asleep. I want to thank Him for helping me see myself, and work through me to help others. I also want to thank myself. I feel great today, as I have come from dark places that could have prevented me from going further and seeing the great world I see today. I thank myself for recognizing the pains, having the courage to deal with them, and having the activation of wisdom to learn from them and stand strong today. Today I give thanks to God.

I also want to thank my grandmother for planting the seed of Jesus in my heart and never giving up on me till the day she took her last breath. I want to thank my mother for never giving up on me and always praying for me. I want to thank my beautiful daughter who has always believed in me despite all we have been through together. I want to thank those that God sent, the staff members and counselors at Mecca. I also want to thank those who took time to plant seeds in my life and water them and all of those who poured into my life and loved me unconditionally. Today I give thanks to my Lord and Savior Jesus Christ.

When I tell you my story, I'm going to refer to all of it as "my version". This is the version I felt deeply, and no one can take this version away from me. Just as no one can take my version away from me, I neither want to take anyone else's version of my story away from them. I understand we all have different perspectives in life, even different perspectives from the same situations, and today I am okay with that. I will not claim that someone else's truths are not factual, simply because I have a different interpretation or recollection of said "truth". We all must deal with life's terms in a way that helps us understand truth.

I was very pretty as a little girl. I remember my heart would fill with warmth and comfort when I would hear little girls are "full of sugar and spice and everything nice." I loved wearing pretty, little dresses and playing with Barbie dolls that had long hair. I was always smiling until around the tender age of 8. You know, sometimes things change for the worse, and at this time, it was definitely where my life started to shift. The energy of the people around us will have an overwhelming power that we can grow from or be a victim of. I became a victim to so many people and their ways. My smiles often faded quickly during these next few traumatic years. I will be way into adulthood years before the next time I will get a piece of what a peace of mind feels like.

After turning 8, my life turned very hard and cold. Let me take you back before I was a God-fearing woman on a mission to change the lives of others and create betterment for my surroundings. Let me take you back to the pretty little girl that dreamed of being a model. I had long pretty hair, and my skin was lighter than most Blacks I was around. I was born in Des Moines, IA. I believe my brain has blocked a lot of my memory from my earlier years for protection. I don't remember a lot from that time period. I don't remember birthday parties or anything fun of that sort. It wasn't long before I wasn't the only child, so my days of being spoiled were short. As I was caught up in being the most beautiful little girl with my Barbie dolls, here comes my siblings. My little brother and sister came to join me. I had a horrible relationship with my little sister; however, my brother and I were very close. I would protect him because that's what big sisters do.

Being the oldest sibling, I had more tasks added to my responsibilities. Since I was the oldest with added responsibilities, I acted and felt like my two siblings were my kids. I felt like I had to grow up quickly because my time was spent feeding, cleaning and cooking for my brother and sister. Even though the time period is very faint, there were still a few vivid memories I have as a younger child.

One of those memories was always talking to my grandmother. Our relationship was full of love, and she had a strong relationship with God. If you were around my grandmother at any given moment, trust and believe you would have heard about the Lord. She loved God so much. Her love of

God was very influential. I learned a lot about God and life when listening to my grandmother. However, I didn't understand why I was forced to stay with her for a portion of my childhood. My mother didn't want to deal with me anymore, but my father was living in town as well, so why couldn't I stay with him? I didn't feel wanted by my dad since I would only see him periodically, but at this time I didn't understand why I wouldn't have stayed with him instead. I explain later why this wasn't an option. My rebellious actions and foul mouth made it hard for the adults in my life to deal with me, so I remember feeling inadequate because my siblings were home with my mother, but I was ostracized and bounced around to different places.

Another memory I have is being at King Elementary school. I was an easy target for bullying and being laughed at. Why? Because I was a girl who had boy clothes. We didn't have a lot of money and it showed because I had to get hand me downs from my bigger boy family. I was humiliated several times to the point I would try to skip school. I hated school. I would have my head down as I walked, not understanding my beauty and the power I possessed from within. I would want to go hide far away from these boys and girls that would laugh at my tomboyish and silly inadequate wardrobe. I would remember questioning myself, "I'm a girl, so why do

I have on boy clothes?" It was very awkward to me that I was not wearing normal "girl" clothes like all the other girls that were around me. There were plenty of times when I did dress like a girl, and that brought me joy and a little bit of normalcy. But oftentimes, I was just uncomfortable from either my clothes not fitting right or just not feeling accepted. This is one experience I remember and thought about quite a bit over the years. Experiences like this help shape and mold our thoughts as we grow older. We learn to internalize and interpret life through our own customized meanings, from the world we come from. As you read my story, please be open to stepping into my shoes and take what you can use for your benefit and leave the rest. I share my story in hopes to help in someone's healing process. I share my story because I know I'm not alone and I want to help where I can. The journey I have traveled was meant for me to live today with a message of hope to all who will listen. Up until this moment as I write, everything that I went through in life was meant to be, and I am grateful for my story and my life. I'm also grateful for your life, and the precious time you are spending becoming more familiar with me and the road I traveled.

There are moments in our lives that are monumental to us. Some of us may have hundreds, some of us may only hold a few of these moments. However, life is filled with refreshing moments that can give you energy for short to extended periods of time and will carry us through the turbulence of tough times. These moments help us get past the hurt and pain caused by other darker moments in our lives.

One of the bright moments in my life was when I got my first pair of white capris pants. I was eleven years old, and I had not had new clothes in a long time so when my mother bought me these cute white pants and a white shirt, I was in heaven. You know when you have the fresh outfit laid out the night before school, thinking to yourself how fresh you are going to be? Well, that was my moment. I remember her sitting me down on the floor and putting ponytails in my hair. I felt wanted as I was putting on my new fresh white Capri pants, white shirt, and white tennis shoes. I also remember walking out of the front door of the apartment on my way to school. I felt whole. I felt loved, and I felt very pretty. I felt loved because my mother sat me down and showed me some genuine undivided attention and brushed my hair. I felt important that my mother took the time to make me feel good. I smiled throughout that day often. I walked with my head held high, and my strut was on point! I remember vividly how warm I felt sitting on our floor getting my hair done. I was being catered to and it felt so special. The journey I have traveled was meant for me to share to all who will listen. To tell you of God's grace, hope and to never give up.

What I am hoping that you receive from this book is plenty. You will gather a lot of gratitude, grace, and most importantly power. Gratitude for being wherever you are in life at this moment. You are more than who you were yesterday, and you can be more than you are today, tomorrow. Grace would come from self-reflecting and realizing you are where you are today because of where you were and what you did yesterday. Life is full of lessons, stresses, trials, and tribulations and then death. During these lessons and stresses, you walk through life and coming one day you will wake up with a sense of POWER. You will think to yourself, and honestly believe that everything will be okay no matter what happens. No matter what comes along that unravels, you will be strong and experienced enough to mend "it" and put it back together. You have fought some storms in your previous days, so when you see a storm today, you won't curl up in a ball and try to hide. Understand the storms come not to break you, they come to make you. Living life on life's terms takes experience, patience and believing you can and walking by faith. You will not avoid your issues and obstacles, because instead you will make life happen.

Power grows in you. Living life on life's own terms takes experience, patience, and a sense of faith from something higher than you. This is my story and I want to share my truths with you. James 1:2-8 "My brethren, count it all joy when you fall into various trials, 3 knowing that the testing of your faith produces (a) patience. 4 But let patience have its perfect work, that you may be (b) perfect and complete, lacking nothing. 5 if any of you lacks wisdom, let him ask of God, who give to us liberally and without reproach, and it will be given to him."

The Birth

Born to my parents, Violet, and Leon, on April 18, 1971. My childhood was very blurry. I do not remember a lot about anything. I do not remember birthday celebrations, nor enjoying family parties or anything close to a party. I can say I remember vividly having a yearning love for my father but being disappointed repeated early from his constant absence. My mother was the stable one, but she always worked. We did not have a typical strong bond because we didn't grow close, so we never grew comfortable around each other. I still loved my mother, even though she screamed a lot! She had absolutely no patience. She was frequently very upset, and I would see her cry a lot and feel very disappointed. Years later I now see what disappointment and heartbreak look and feel like, and I often think back to moments that make me think my mother felt the same way back then. She may have been feeling her heartbreaks over the years.

At the time, when I was younger, I felt the tension and the brokenness, but I couldn't understand why or what it was.

Being a parent is the most challenging task ever. We don't know a lot of the challenges we face and how to deal with them. We still must be a parent regardless of how we are feeling internally. By the time you become a parent, you already have seen a lot of traumas and ills that affect your mindset, and interpretation of the world. We spend years trying to figure out life. Unfortunately, we tend to learn ourselves in the last stages of our lives. We tend to learn all about who we are AFTER we spend years trying to figure out life and raise our children. So, during the time of us being parents, we give it our all, but our all is not always the best because we aren't physically, emotionally, or mentally able to give optimal effort. We only give the best we can under our circumstances.

I feel like my mother had a dream of what her adulthood would look like, but for some reason she was disappointed because her life didn't look at all how she thought it would look when she was younger. I think she was very hard working and was always working. She seemed like she never was comfortable with our situation though. She always wanted more for us, but we just didn't have it. I didn't feel comfort from her, but I did feel a sense of security and stability. My mother worked one job, came home for a brief second and would get on to the next one. She made sure my siblings and I had what we needed. To this day I am grateful for being a witness to my mother's work ethic. She really did what she had to do. I would always wonder why my mother was so cold towards me. It was stress. She was very distant. I remember wishing she would hug me tight and tell me she loved me. Being older now and traveling upon my own journey, I can see how a woman can turn to being a hard and cold soul. I get it, and I hold no ill will towards my mother as she was doing the best she could do. She still didn't like me though. Or it appeared that way to me.

I had to go stay at grandma's house because she didn't want to deal with me anymore. She said I was a troublemaker. Well wouldn't you be if you were confused and mad? I had reason to be both. First, it seemed like I was being touched by every older boy that was around me. I had a couple of older cousins that were really having their way with me in my early years. It was tough and to avoid these cousins, at times I would make sure I peed on myself when he would come around so he wouldn't touch me. When I peed on myself, this would guarantee that I could rest alone that night because he would think I was dirty and smelled bad. I didn't know what else to do. I didn't tell my mother because he was my mother's favorite nephew. I don't think she would have believed me. I didn't want my cousin getting in trouble because at that young age, I didn't know if it was wrong or not. I loved him. I was taught to love family and that is what I did. My cousin was a lot older than me. I was only nine. I didn't like what he would do to me though it got to the point where I would run and hide in closets as well because I would try to avoid this guy's touch. During this time period, I grew very defiant and unruly. I would be rebellious on purpose. I turned into a very angry child. Who wouldn't become angry after being violated often? Who wouldn't be confused?

My dad would pop up maybe twice a year. I would go and stay with him from time to time. He had a wife that didn't like me. I believe she didn't like me because I was the "poor little black girl" that came from my mother. I had a half sister and I feel she was treated way better than me because she was half white.

At night, I would hear the screams from his wife. Alcohol was no friend of my dad's because he overindulged. He was a true alcoholic. When he did, he would beat his wife, my stepmother. I only remember my father being abusive towards his wife and him being very evasive towards me. He treated me like a stepchild. He never gave or showed love for me. I believe to this day the only reason he ever took time for me was to satisfy his own shame and guilt of not ever really caring for me.

During these times of him beating on my stepmother, my stepsister and I would run and hide in the nearby cubby that was on the wall. Then we wouldn't hear my stepmother screaming. It was always late at night. He would come home late after drinking and pick a fight with his wife and beat her. He would yell and carry on as if he were a hurt little boy inside. I remember thinking, "why is he so angry?" I also started to believe that beating women is just what men do.

It is crazy that our younger years are full of learning and soaking up everything we see like a sponge. However, these years, what we see in our childhoods are so crucial to our outward look at the world as we get older. I look back and see why I accepted the abuse in my own life as I got older. One time I came downstairs early morning and I saw my stepmother in the kitchen cooking. She would not turn around and look at us kids, but when she did, I saw two black eyes. She looked so sad. We were speechless. I didn't know what to think. Meanwhile at my mother's house, another blended family was created. My mother had a short-lived boyfriend who became my stepdad. He did not like me either. I remember asking myself why doesn't anyone like me? I believe my mother knew he didn't like me, but she dealt with him and the awkwardness of the situation because he was a great provider. I believe she wanted us to have a good life, and in her eyes, he was the key to this since he was a construction worker that worked very hard.

If someone was to ask me to describe my childhood in one word, it would be a no brainer. I would not even blink an eye as I yelled the word "rejection"! Rejection is the root of my pains and is an experience that came around quite often as a child. For me, I hated rejection. As a child, I felt like I didn't belong anywhere because I was rejected from everyone. I didn't understand why I wasn't liked by my family, but often I felt my presence was not wanted. I felt pretty at times, and I believed pretty little girls were treasures for the world, but I didn't fit in that category. At 10 years old, my thoughts were all about not being on earth anymore. I wanted to die. I would think to myself, "I wonder if anyone would even miss me if I died." The only people that I didn't feel like hated me was the ones that touched on me, and that was very confusing for me as a little girl.

Being rejected and ostracized by family at a young age is very bad to deal with. Even in later years, certain things from my past trigger me and the feeling of rejection can take me down a dark place if I don't counter the feelings with a unique perspective. I've grown over the years to have a mechanism that combats the rejection feeling. Now God has a different route for me to go and being rejected is now more like being protected and steering clear from what can potentially hurt me. I now realize that rejection is God not only protecting me but taking me a new direction. I wish I would have understood this at 10. Instead at that time, rejection pushed me to rebel and fight my feelings of confusion. I was 10 years old and was getting touched on by my cousin. I was feeling like every adult around me just didn't want me around. I watched my dad beat my stepmother, who couldn't stand me. I would think "why does she hate me? She should hate my dad for giving her black eyes, not me."

During this same time of this pre-teen stage of my life, I developed a tough attitude after watching my mother be an extreme pushover to my stepdad. At the time, I saw a woman that didn't fight back and let people walk all over her. I told myself I would never be that person, and this created conflict in my world. Backing down was not my cup of tea. I wanted to stand up for my mother and stand up for myself specially to prove to my mother that we don't have to take any crap. I felt my mother was a big pushover and I understand now, I just didn't agree with it then. I watched my stepdad run the household because he was a hard worker and made lots of money. He took care of the bills and my mother thought she was doing the right thing to keep him. My stepdad didn't like me. He would tell my mother I was disrespectful and rebellious because he didn't like my boldness. I was 10- and 11-years old feeling like I had to step up for my mother else he would run all over us. I thought I was smarter than everyone around me, but I was very upset with the world. I was being touched on and I felt rejection from everyone in my family. I remember being 10 and 11 thinking to myself, "If I just died, nobody would even care." I would contemplate committing suicide repeatedly.

This time of my life was very hard because I would really feel like no matter what I did, I was rejected. Therefore, I would stand up to my stepdad. I felt like I needed a way to get attention, whether it was good or bad attention. He would yell at me when I would stick up for my mother. I pushed so hard to get attention, I got pushed right on out of my mother's house. My stepdad didn't want me to be there anymore, so my mother sent me to live with my paternal grandmother. I remember staying there and her house was always so cold. I would freeze over there. I didn't like staying there because I could tell I really wasn't wanted there. She treated my half-sister better than me. I felt like it was because she was half white and I was made by mistake. No one else wanted me and I guess she took me because she felt sorry for me. She never showed me love. Looking back, it was so artificial. During that time my paternal aunt decided I needed therapy because I was just a messed-up kid. She felt therapy was the answer. It's a fond memory of my childhood to have this therapist. She told me I was beautiful and smart. This was a first that stuck with me. I remember thinking no one ever told me that. It was easy for me to think I was the child nobody wanted. I always saw my siblings being taken care of and comfortable. Me, on the other hand was tossed around and stuck wherever I could stick for a while. But when she told me I was beautiful, I smiled. When she told me I was smart, I couldn't believe it. Here is this woman that doesn't know anything about me, and she is telling me I'm smart. No one ever told me that so it must have been her job to tell me this. I thought of all types of reasons why she told me that, and I would believe them all except maybe she really thought I was smart and beautiful. But I sure didn't feel like it. I felt like a stepchild who was abandoned because no one wanted me, not even my own mother.

At this stage of my life, I was going on a downhill spiral. My thoughts started to shape my views of the world and they turned me down a negative path. I didn't have anyone there to check me, and I didn't have the confidence to check my own negative ways of thinking. It is important for kids to have those positive reinforcing statements about them from the ones they love. "You can do anything you put your mind to because you are smart." "Look at how you did that! You are awesome! Excellent job!", or "it is ok that you messed up, we all do. Pick up the pieces and try again. Keep going!" I didn't have any of that besides this white lady that was getting paid to tell me these things. So obviously I adopted and trained myself into having a negative outlook about myself. I thought I was lower than everyone else. I felt like I was different, and I didn't even fit in with my family. This was hard for me for the next several years. I spent years trying to overcome the feeling of rejection by trying to find love in several different toxic relationships. I started out my quest to finding love with an awfully terrible experience when I lost my virginity "by choice". I say by choice because this was the first time, I had sex by my own free will and choice. I gave my virginity away to a boy that I was seeing for a while. He made me feel good. We were both 13 at the time. When I say he made me feel good, he listened to me and didn't judge me. He said he liked me, and I believed him. The sexual experience was terrible, but it didn't discourage me from trying repeatedly.

During middle school, I was sent to live with my father in Southern California. There I was thrown into a household which consisted of my father, his wife and an older stepbrother, who was gay and very mean to me. He would hit me when no one else was around, but no one believed me. I was seen as the poor little black girl that started trouble everywhere I went so no one saw me as credible. My father worked during the day and by night he was an abusive alcoholic, so we didn't really spend a lot of time together. We barely spoke to each other. This short-lived time of my life in California ended, which I knew it would. My father grew tired of me and sent me back to my mother. On my way back to Iowa, I began to feel even more depressed. Anyone that has experienced California living, and then comes back to the Midwest can see and feel a significant difference. The weather in California was so nice and refreshing. You didn't have to worry about snow and gloomy weather, as the saying goes "it never rains in Southern California." As I look back at this time, I can see how the weather played a role in my downward spiral.

When I finally got back to Des Moines, and its gloomy nature, I became extremely defiant and rebellious. I was 13 years old and felt the world was out to get me. Currently, I was an incredibly angry girl. I felt that all the men in my life were either wanting to touch on me, or they just didn't care about me. The women in my life didn't like me. My mother was a pushover and I hated that about her. I felt nobody loved me enough to want to teach me and be there for me. I was broken!

My heart was full of pain and disappointment. I didn't know anything about life besides it was hard, and everyone seemed to be happy and normal besides me. I didn't know what love was, but I swear I was trying to find it in many places. Then I decided to start running away often. At 13, I was running around town sleeping with different guys so I could have a place to stay. School wasn't a priority for me, and no one was making me go, so it didn't matter. I would steal my stepdad's car a few times. I imagine this didn't help him feel any better about me. He didn't like me, and I understand why he didn't, now that I am grown and can look back at my mistakes. How can you blame me for being so rebellious? Look at everything I was going through in life. I would often question God and ask why He would allow my life to be this way. Being out on the streets at 13 with a kid's sense of direction seemed like a curse, and definitely not a gift.

Fast forward to 14 and now I am pregnant with my first child. My boyfriend at the time was not excited. I felt this was a time where we could love each other, but at 14 who would understand love and becoming a parent at the same time. Becoming a mother changed me, as it does most women. The father was a little bit older than me. He was kind of mean, but I was used to the males in my life being mean, so I didn't stress about that. In a weird way, I expected him to be mean.

I think at that time I thought I was being loved. But after he beat me, I had to go. I couldn't deal with that and didn't want to. Shortly after I left him, I met another guy by the name of Chris. He was eight years older than me, but I didn't care. He was like a father figure. He convinced me he was like a father to me, and he controlled my every move. He would beat me all the time. I stayed and endured the pain because I thought I was in love and at the time, it felt like he was proving to me that he loved me. We also lived with his mother and father at the time. I just couldn't understand why his parents would allow him to be with a 14-year-old little girl. He was 21. Now as I look back and reflect, I see why now. After I had my baby boy, I had Chris convinced the baby was his. I thought he would treat me better if he believed that, but he still beat me. His mother allowed it, and his father ignored it. I remember many times hearing his mother say to me, "well if you would just shut up, he wouldn't beat you." I started to think this was just normal behavior. In a way, even though his mother didn't like me, and I didn't like her, I looked up to her. She was an older role model that I had in front of me, so I tried to respect her, but she was just too nasty towards me. I felt I didn't have any other options, I couldn't stay with my mother, my father didn't want me there, so I guess I had to deal with my life being the way it was. He started to beat me daily, and it felt as if he was doing it for approval from his mother. See, hatred is passed down and taught. Chris inherited this hatred from his mother. It's like his mother was punishing me through him. He also looked up to his mother and I can tell he was seeking validation from her. It's like the meaner he was to me and everyone else, the more she loved and respected him. As I'm older now, I see this more and more. However, unfortunately at that time I had to be the victim and all I could see and pay attention to at that time was my own cries for help. I felt hopeless. His mother was a drug addict. She turned to drugs because of her traumatized life and experiences. She too was abused, and drugs are a way to deal with escaping your life that you don't like and become numb into a world that you can't feel. Her drug usage trickled down to Chris as well. Even though at the time I didn't know or understand drug use, I was around it every day and had no clue. Chris was a crack addict along with his mother and father. They were using me for food stamps and other benefits I would get for being a young mother. I was trading being beaten and food stamps for a place to stay, which for some reason I still felt grateful. Chris would cheat on me over and over and one time when I was eight months pregnant, I walked in on him cheating on me in the basement of his mother's house. His mother knew exactly what he was doing, and he then immediately beat me badly.

The Struggle

A month after walking in on Chris cheating on me, my world changed when I delivered my baby boy into the world. I was 15 years old. I looked at him and was instantly in love! I became a mother! What a beautiful time. I would hold him and stare at him. He was born healthy even though I was beaten and stressed the entire pregnancy, but God created perfection. He was beautiful with silky black hair and fair skin like mine. As I would spend hours holding him, I would sing Anita Baker's "you bring me joy" (google the song if you don't know it, so you can know what I felt) with tears in my eyes. I dreamed of how I would provide for him and love him. I felt loved by him from the moment I saw him.

At this moment, I believed that since I was the mother to Chris's child and to his mother's grandchild, they would love me now as well. Well, that didn't happen. I think me having the baby added fuel to their burning hatred for me. I feel Chris was more controlling and demanding, and his mother felt I was a bad mom. Every chance she had, she would try and take my baby from me.

I convinced Chris that we need our own place and he agreed. Shortly after our baby was born, we went and found a place. It was a cute little one-bedroom apartment that I loved because it was ours, and I was proud that we could afford it and take care of ourselves. After being together for a little longer, I wound up pregnant again. During this time period away from his mother's house, Chris would still rape and beat me. I remember him the day I gave birth to my second son, I found myself screaming for him to stop raping me. After his vigorous rant and tantrum, I went into labor a couple of hours later. Shortly after I had his baby, he beat me unconscious. I could hear everything around me, but I couldn't feel my body. When I woke up the next day, he was standing over me telling me he loved me. What kind of life is this? What did I do to deserve this? This isn't the love I want and have been actively seeking since I can remember. I am being tortured. So, our baby boy came prematurely 6 weeks (about 1 and a half months) early due to Chris hitting and raping me hours before I went into labor.

Chris promised he would never hit me again. I wanted to believe him, and I was very happy for this. Half of me trusted him and the other half thought he was full of it. I heard similar from him before. Sometimes we went to believe things so bad that we our clouded from good judgment. I gave him an opportunity because I wanted us to work and be happy as a family. But Chris turned into a man that never was around. He just added to my stress levels. I had postpartum depression, anxiety, stress, and feeling hopeless. Chris would work all week, get his paycheck on Friday and I wouldn't see him until Sunday. He would come home Sunday night and then the routine would repeat itself over and over. I was 16, and alone with two babies. Talk about not knowing what to do. I was lost. I was so mad at myself for getting in this situation, but I loved my kids. I felt it was just me and them against the world, including Chris. I felt Chris was against me the most. But how? I was the mother of his children. I would think he would have a love and respect for me like no other.

Let's talk more about his addiction. First, I really feel his mother encouraged him to be an addict and abuser. She was the one that started him on drugs. She gave him his first line of cocaine. The hateful ways she displayed day to day, it's hard for me to believe she has a speck of goodness in her cold heart. She has a bitter outlook on life, so how can she want happiness for anyone else? That's how that usually works. Miserable people don't wish happiness and prosperity for others, regardless of it being family. However, Chris's crack cocaine addiction was escalating quickly. I imagine he was extremely stressed trying to figure out this parenting thing, and he never knew a different coping mechanism besides what he had seen his mother and father do. At the time I couldn't focus on his problems, I had to raise these babies and I couldn't quit. At the height of Chris's addiction, he faked a burglary to our home. Addiction will have you manipulating and conniving your way through life and hurting anyone close to you regardless how much you love them. It's truly sad to watch someone go down the road of chemical dependency because there's nothing you can do for them until it's time for them to say, "enough is enough". We want their recovery more than they do at times. We must realize, sometimes the reason for their addiction is their defense. An addict is protecting him or her from their own feelings, or their own disappointments. They may be heartbroken, and the drug takes them away from that pain. When we are on the outside looking in, we don't understand everything that is going on in their head. We don't see the guilt they may have from their past. We don't see the tears of heartbreak from a loved one. We don't see the pain from a loved one passing. All we see is their destruction of self, and we want better for them.

One day during my loneliness and frustrations of being a "single" mother with two kids, I decided to leave the apartment for a little bit. This meant that I would get a quick breather from the kids after being cooped up with them for days on end. All I remember was feeling like I needed a break for just an hour. Lord, just give me an hour to myself. Chris was never at home and all I've seen for a week straight is diapers, sippy cups, and hearing babies' cry. Chris had decided to join the Army reserves in Colorado and felt that doing that would help him get clean. I still don't know how he passed the drug screen, but he entered the Army. It was very draining! I waited for both of my babies to fall asleep, and I made a dash to the door. I put a butter knife in the door to keep them from coming out the door while I was gone. I got back about an hour later and both of my kids were gone. This was a bad mistake I had made. A friend came over while I was gone and heard the babies crying inside. My friend took the babies to my mother's house and my stepdad wouldn't let them stay. Now this situation got the Department of Human Services (DHS) in the mix.

Unfortunately, Chris and his mother told them I am an unfit parent. How is it that two crack addicts, and one of them being a physical abuser, would be able to convince DHS that I was a bad mother? Me being young and naïve, I really didn't know how to fight that fight. All I was concerned with was my babies being stuck with Chris and his mother, and I would hate for them to treat them the way they treated me. I asked DHS for them to be put into foster care. I'd rather them to be raised by anyone besides them two. I was begging for DHS to not allow these devils to raise my babies. Well DHS didn't listen, and next thing you know I am in the middle of a power trip. Chris came back from Denver and hired an attorney and was given placement of my children. Anytime I wanted to see my kids, I would have to have sex with Chris. Him and his mother just took full control and used my own children against me. I wondered why they hated me so much. What was it about me that made people just want to be downright mean? I swear I wasn't a bad person. I didn't like conflict. But the way my life was going, everyone involved besides my two children were against me. And now the two people that hate me are raising my children?

To add more confusion and chaos to my life, as time went on, I grew close to Chris and at 17, he asked to marry me. I said yes. The day we got married, while in his mother's basement, he beat me. No one reached out to stop this marriage. None of my family batted an eye. They knew he was beating me. They knew he tortured me and used my kids against me. But what am I to do? I didn't have anywhere to turn. My own mother wasn't going to help me. At 17, Chris and his devilish mother were the only ones that gave me a sense of belonging, even though it wasn't healthy for me. So here I am, a high school dropout with 2 kids. I'm married to a crackhead who is beating me every chance he gets, and his mother has turned my own kids against me. My family has abandoned me, and I'm all alone with no friends. I was desperate. I didn't know what I was going to do but I knew that I wasn't going to stay where I was getting beat on. I had enough of that. I built up the courage to leave this man and I got my own place, but I also started running the streets. I met tons of people that seemed to be in similar situations. A few people started teaching me how to hustle and get money, so I took to it all quickly. I started writing bad checks and after a few times, I got caught and ended up in jail for nine months.

Sitting in jail will have you thinking and reevaluating your whole life. But I wasn't done with the fast life. Matter of fact, I was just getting started. I ended up going back to Chris. I was missing my babies, and I was missing him as well. I realized Chris and his mother were using my kids and telling them I didn't love them. How can someone be that cruel to kids? I knew this would happen when they took over custody.

When I went back to Chris, I realized his drug addiction was getting worse. He would smoke more and more crack, and he was just becoming dirtier. His hygiene was starting to be poor. He was more abusive verbally as well. I met a friend one night and she invited me to Minnesota with her. I jumped at the opportunity. Well, she wasn't going for a vacation, she was going to work. This is when my life changed.

(JoJo)

Going to Albert Lea, Minnesota with Shelly changed my life. On the way there, she bragged about how much money she was getting for "just dancing" in front of these old men. I didn't believe it for one bit. She said, "just you wait, you will see". We entered the bar about 9:30 one Saturday night. I didn't have any intentions on dancing, I was just going to observe and hang out. I ended up dancing on top of the bar, but I still had most of my clothes on. While I was dancing, this middle aged balding white man comes up to me. He appeared to be a wealthy guy, and very clean cut. His sandy brown hair was thinning in the middle, but he was confident. I could tell by the way he walked he knew he had it going on. He would give me some money if I didn't take any more of my clothes off and I wipe the red lipstick off my face. He starts throwing money at me. "You are way too pretty to be taking your clothes off for strangers." He kept throwing money my way and saying the same thing over and over. I just kept smiling and dancing. By the time the song went off and I was done with my first routine, I walked off the stage with $ 5,000 dollars. I couldn't believe it. You can say that turned me out! I was ready for this life, and I was turned out from that point forward. You couldn't tell me this wasn't the way out of my situation. You couldn't tell me this wasn't the way for me to raise my kids, start me a business and get my life together. I never had that much money in my life and to think I danced for less than 10 minutes. I was so excited. The man that paid me all that money became one of my regulars, and from then on he spent a lot of money on me. Donald, the middle-aged, balding white man loved him some JoJo. He never got too personal with me, but I believe his wife had passed. He was a lonely man that had a lot of money. I met so many men in these clubs that were like Donald. Not all these men were the stereotypical old horny men that were desperate for sex. So many of these men would trade their hard-earned dollars for conversations. I grew accustomed to plenty of platonic, innocent companionship relationships where I didn't have to do anything indecent. These situations demanded a lot of my time, but more of my intriguing thoughts. I couldn't imagine paying someone top dollars just to be around someone to talk to. But these men were few and far between the rest of the fast life.

For the next 17 years, I was living a very fast life. The journey of this phase of my life made me grow to who I am today. My name wasn't Joanna anymore, it was JoJo the Dancer. I loved what I was doing for the first year or so. I just felt the power I had on stage from my body, and the power I had off stage with my money. Traveling up and down the highways, adventuring from one club to the next was hard work that took devotion and a lot of energy. All the way around, day in and day out, I was living a dream. On stage, I was loved for those moments. The sense of rejection was nonexistent. JoJo was somebody! JoJo had the men bowing down to her off and on stage. That alter ego was something else. For that first year, I was high on life. I would travel from South Dakota, Chicago, Omaha, and everywhere in between. I was a traveling superstar. Anyone in the dancing world in those cities knew who JoJo was. I was moving and shaking all over the Midwest making tons of money and partying. When you are young with no direction, sometimes money is the worst thing you can have. I didn't know what to do with all the money I was making, but I do know that an array of habits can be easily formed when you have the money to support them. While I was living the fast life for that first year, it was fun and addicting. It was that way for the next seven years.

I settled down at a local strip club in Des Moines and became a house dancer. I became a regular house girl at one of the oldest and most consistent strip clubs in Iowa. This is when this dancing thing turned into a job. Anyone that knows me knows how I didn't like the thought of a job. The main difference in becoming a house dancer as opposed to a traveling one, you lose more of the control. When you travel, you are the "fresh meat, or new thing. If you don't like one club and the personalities that one club comes with, you can leave and never go back. It's easy to club hop and be somewhere better the next day. When you become a house dancer, you become a servant to your clientele that you must build. A lot of times those guys that would pay me big money weren't able to come see me in other cities. The money I would get from my regulars would keep me around the club that I really didn't like, around personalities that I did not get along with. It was also the same old thing night in and night out. If you are like me, you like variety and moving around. The scene at this club I was working at was becoming more and more difficult for me to enjoy. I started to need motivation. While as a house dancer at this club, I met Troy and got pregnant. We married, but he was also an abuser. I don't speak on this short-lived relationship and time frame too often because it isn't a different significant part of my life. I love my daughter though. I'm glad I had her. I left Troy shortly after my daughter was born. I began to get used to large sums of money on me. Even though I wasn't great with money, I still wanted the opportunity to blow it, and if I didn't have it, I felt in a bad way. Money kept me on an emotional roller coaster and getting up coming to make money felt like work. I felt like I was punching a clock and wasn't as free as I wanted to be. I turned to drugs to allow me to escape the dryness of my routine.

Now, throughout my first year of dancing at this club, I watched people shoot up, smoke dope on foil, do meth, pills etc. You name it, I saw these dancers indulge right before they went on stage to escape and really take the feelings out of their next moves. It's hard to continuously throw your body on stage and walk-through drooling, lust-filled men day in and day out, participating in these activities, so I understood the reasons these women did these things. Drugs created your escape of the reality of what was really happening. I finally gave in to the pressures of this fast world and I started experimenting with my colleagues. I tried meth, and I didn't like it. I tried weed, didn't like how paranoid I got. I literally thought everyone around me was the police. I was very uncomfortable. Tried cocaine and said to myself, "this is it! I can do this." The euphoria I felt with cocaine made it so desirable, and so easily addicted. Not only did the numbness to reality cocaine creates feel so good, but it also helped me regulate my weight. As a dancer, keeping a consistent well-shaped figure as your body is your money-maker, and just as important as your gift to gab, or mouthpiece. Conversations rule the nations, but you must be eye candy to these men, else they will cast you aside and get to looking at the next dancer that walks by with glitter, a big butt and a smile.

Now as my addiction to cocaine started to increase, my hustle got stronger. I worked more hours, took less days off and started to spend more money on the road back and forth from Des Moines to Omaha. This is where my life started to turn even more into some challenging times. The money from dancing was great. At this point of my addiction, I didn't have to do anything but put my hand out, and I would get a gram or two. I had several sugar daddy's that distributed cocaine. These sugar daddies were hurting me by enabling me to do as much cocaine as I wanted. My self- destruction hadn't started yet, but those days were coming. I started to have cocaine every day. I had so many resources to get it whenever, so I didn't realize how it was taking over because I wasn't spending money on it. At one point, I thought highly of myself and better than everyone else because I convinced myself I was better because "I wasn't buying it." What an illusion that was. I started snorting quite a bit at a time. In my head I looked beautiful, but looking back at that time period, I looked very thin, face sunken in and stressed. But the drugs kept me going strong and up and down the highway chasing money, fame, the life, and at this point, the most important thing, cocaine.

The fast life is exciting at the beginning. You're meeting new people, making money, and getting introduced to so many new things. But the drugs take over. Some people get taken over quicker than others, but when it grips you, it's almost impossible to shake it off you. During my addiction, as it grew deeper and deeper, I started to abandon my kids. In return, I would abandon them more because I was feeling shameful and guilty for doing the drugs and falling so low. But just when you thought the low couldn't get any lower, it did.

Devastation of Dancing

The money was getting so good, I started working only two nights a week. Other nights I would work at a local urban nightclub as a bartender. I felt miserable inside. I felt like I chose the life of a dancer over my kids. There was a point in time where I felt as if money was the only thing that mattered, and my kids had everything the ever needed. I showered my kids with gifts, and everything they ever wanted, but at the cost of valuable time. If I could go back and change the hands of time, I would square up and get a job where I could slow down and focus on my kids. If I were to do that, my daughter would have more respect for me, and one of my sons wouldn't have turned to the gang life at an early age. I felt so bad because my sons developed an alcohol addiction. I felt like I failed as a mother. All I did for years was chase the money and drugs, and provide a financial home, but I didn't support my kids mentally. I wasn't there for them during these dark times. I wanted to do better; I really did! That was all I thought about and I worried so heavily about my sons being hurt out in the streets. I worried about having a better relationship with my daughter, but these drugs had a hold on me. I would worry myself into more drugs to hide from the pain of feeling like a bad mom. This vicious cycle had me spiraling downhill all the time. I would often wonder what else I could do in life besides dance. Yeah, on stage when I'm JoJo, I am the center of it all. I'm the center of attention and the focus in the room. I attracted a kind of man that I didn't even respect. I just gave them what they needed in order to get what I needed. In over 17 years of dancing, I would say the last 10 of those years, I was high the entire time. There was no way I could do a job like this sober. Night in and night out sped by so fast, I was now in the present realization that I failed these years. My kids were the result of my failing them. Yes, we had a beautiful home, with all the latest gadgets and spacious room. But it was up to me to make it feel like a home. It was just a place we stayed at, and I beat myself up about that. Growing up, the home you are in impacts you.

One night I'm out with the kiddos at a local pet store getting some hay for the house, and I met the man of my dreams. We were standing waiting for two bales of hay, and this guy was standing in the back of the line. He just so happened to be buying bales of hay as well. I go outside and one of the workers pulls around these bales of hay and suddenly, I realize that I cannot haul these two big bales in my little car. What was I thinking? Well, it was so ironic when that gorgeous man I had my eyes on in the store came outside to his big ol' pickup truck, and threw his bales in the back with ease, and proceeded to get in his truck. Totally innocent, I thought quick and asked this man to bring my bales of hay to my house. He obliged, and twenty minutes later we were talking outside of my house about everything. I had butterflies. I'm sure he could see how I was choosing him, because my body language could not lie. I was open. He tells me he is a carpenter and does a lot of fixings around the house, and I fell in love. I was looking at this man as if he was heaven sent. In my mind he was the Prince Charming I needed. Here I am making all this money, kids growing like weeds and my house is falling apart around me. It needed order and structure, and a strong man could bring a foundation. He appeared to be a hard worker. We exchanged numbers and the next several weeks, Craig became a part of my life.

After 3 beautiful months, we got married. Quick, huh? We were in love, so we thought. Well, my daughter didn't like him at all. He and my oldest son had a special bond because they were affiliated with the same gang. Come to find out, this man wasn't only a hard-working carpenter, but he sold crack cocaine. Craig was also a womanizer and had women all over the place. On top of the continuous cheating, he also failed to mention he had a baby on the way prior to us getting married. So here we are in the first year of marriage, and this broke my heart. Again! A broken heart that I was left to mend at some point. His infidelity was devastating to me. Here we were, married and living great and then BOOM! I was a stay-at-home spouse and he worked. This was like a dream come true and then it was a nightmare. He changed quickly and I had no trust left. I wanted to be in love and give this man my all, but after going through the pain of being cheated on over and over, the pain became huge. At this point, I acted my way through the marriage just like I did everything else in my world. I didn't even have a real identity anymore. I didn't know who JoAnna was. I was JoJo 90% of the time. JoJo was a character that was torn apart by the world around her. JoJo was a woman that was hollow, with no feelings. JoAnna hated her, but JoAnna didn't have a strong enough voice to be heard. Now mind you over these 17 years of never being sober, I never touched crack.

One day I was snooping around in Craig's stuff and found his stash of crack. He had a bundle of plastic sandwich bags filled with tiny, yellowish and white rocks. It was a lot of crack, but I had no idea the worth. I went ahead and took a little bit to see what it was all about. Half of me wanted to take it all and throw it away to hurt Craig. But the other half was wanting to escape the reality of my world, and there weren't too many drugs I wouldn't or didn't try.

Well, I got a pipe, crushed up one of those little yellowish white cubes, and smoked it. Oh, it was over! I never felt so extraordinary in my life! I was instantly hooked. I couldn't believe the feeling I had. After about 15 minutes, the high wore off and I immediately took another hit of that dope. I didn't get as high, but it felt so good. I was numb to the world. I was escaping all the filthy men that had touched me over the years. It felt as if my failures as a mother, the men that dogged me, my family that abandoned me, and my self-destructive mindset just disappeared! The pits of my world were deep, and I was stuck, but not within the moments of my high.

Crack Cocaine – My Newfound Lover!

Crack is different. Crack is the ultimate high. You know the saying, "you gotta kick that monkey off your back"? Well crack is a gorilla then. That first time you smoke crack, it is an instant euphoria. You feel incredible for 15 to 20 minutes. You are literally on top of the world. But that feeling is never quite attained again. You spend the rest of your days stealing, scrambling, and maneuvering anything and everything to find that high again, and it's never there. That first mega blast is the most addictive feeling in the world. I spent several years ruining my mind, spirit and body for a high that just couldn't be matched again. My crack habit would have me out manipulating the world. I would sleep with the grimiest of men to get a fix. You go from longing and searching for that first euphoria to just wanting to be high to run from who you have become. Crack will turn you against your loved ones quickly. It didn't take much for me to fall deep into the pits of this powerful drug. It was to the point where I didn't want to snort powder, I didn't want just cocaine. I wanted and needed the cooked form ALL the time.

This was a sticky situation to be in because somehow, I was so slick and sneaky, Craig had no idea I was using his supply. Maybe it wasn't that I was so slick, maybe Craig was moving so fast that he wasn't paying attention enough. He wasn't at home as often and of course he wasn't the family man a wife would be happy with. Craig was out running around making money and chasing women, you know, the typical drug dealer m.o. He didn't have time to notice my mood switches, and the decline of my weight and hygiene. He didn't so much care about my appearance or actions, but I was worried about him finding some of his drugs missing. Craig was very in tune with his money. He knew what was supposed to add up and when numbers didn't add up, everyone around had to feel his wrath. I got paranoid so I started getting my dope from a few of the dealers around Omaha. Omaha was a lot more intense than Des Moines, especially the drug game. You had a lot more dealers, a lot more money and a lot more violence. It wasn't uncommon to see assault rifles on laps of these drug dealers as they drove around the city. Des Moines has and has had its moments, but this was a lot more than I was used to. I would venture over to the North side of Omaha around Ames St. and score big rocks. I hardly ever had to buy crack, because most of the time I could perform some sexual favors. Craig would give me all the cocaine I needed as well, so I would cook it up myself and get high. I was scared to let him know I was smoking crack.

My relationship with Craig was really dwindling. This downward spiral was making it real evident that I had a drug problem. Not only was the arguing and the abuse toxic, but my eating habits were horrible, and I was neglecting my children more. As a result, my son turned to active gang banging, and my daughter was growing more distant. She really hated Craig. She would see us fighting and try to stop us. She would yell at him and throw things at him. We started to fight every day. I realized marrying this man was a mistake.

One New Year's night, Craig and I had a little too much to drink and we started fighting. I feel like fighting was the answer to everything at this point in my life. This was the result of being abused for years. I was emotionally scarred, but I knew I didn't want to take anymore butt whopping from anyone, especially my man. I had enough, and he was going to feel my wrath. I was high on crack as well, so that didn't help me settle down at all. I picked up a knife and something told me to try and kill this man. He lunged at me as I held this knife up, and I struck him across the face. At that point, all I saw was blood trickling out of his face and a phone being thrown across the room. The phone struck my son in the head and now he was bleeding. That night was bad. The next day, I felt the hangover and my body felt like it was throbbing.

After this episode, many months went by, and my son was taken away and put into a boy's home. He was acting out so badly that I put him in the Boys Town of Omaha. In a way, I was happy he was gone because he was way out of hand and was getting to be active in the streets. I didn't want him to get hurt out there, so the boy's home might have been the best thing for him. I worked in a bar in Omaha bartending and that was not a good place for me. Crack was so easy to get at this bar, I felt like I worked in a crack house. The bar was always full of the neighborhood dealers. I could get a little hit anytime I wanted and most of the time for free. They loved JoJo. I played so many little games with all the "ballers", and I thought I was slick. On top of that, all these young money getters were attractive and had it going on. I didn't look at my games I was playing as prostitution, even though it absolutely was. I was giving my body to them for drugs. At that time, I felt as if I was playing them, but now I realize I was playing myself. This all is a part of the crack addiction. It eats at you and makes you lose your common sense. All you think about is getting high. You want more of it and will go to any lengths to get it. Addiction was running rampant in my household. While I was falling apart trying to scheme for every piece of crack I could smoke, my husband was battling his addiction to chasing money and women. His addiction was just as devastating as mine was because he was constantly high. His drug addiction to smoking wet (embalming fluid) was brought on (I believe) from the stresses of chasing money and women at the same time. The ability to sell crack, or any other business endeavor is strained when you add chasing women into the equation. Running around, watching your back, selling drugs, chasing women AND married to a woman that is destroying everything she touches because of her crack habit, that is a tough life to adjust to.

A man that strays from the word of the Lord is in self destruction mode and might not even know it. Then, on top of all that, he found out from the street that I was buying crack from Smooth, a local pusher. That brought on more toxicity in the household. He started beating me even more. This relationship was not going to last much longer. I was spiraling down at a rapid pace. I loved crack! I was selling everything to get and stay high. My life was turning into a drastic mess, and it was getting harder to look like I had it all together. When you are on drugs, no matter how awful you look, you still think you got it going on. You still think you look great and other people can't tell you are falling. Well, you have fallen, it is apparent to everyone you encounter, except you! You don't see it. You think you are fooling everyone when you try and lie. You think you are getting over when you try and manipulate, as well as deceive, but no one is buying your story. Everyone knows before you know when you hit rock bottom.

One night, I come home after the bar, and Craig was standing in the living room naked. He was flipping out, sweating profusely. In his hand he held a Mac 11 machine gun. He had it held to his head ready pull the trigger and leave this earth. My daughter was screaming so loud and hysterically. He then turned the gun on me, and my son jumped in between the gun and my baby girl. She ran to the truck and hid. I remember vividly like it was yesterday. This haunts me to this present day as it plays like a movie through my memory. At this point, I saw my life and my kids' lives flash before my eyes. I felt I had to leave. I've been down this road before and trust me, it wasn't any easier, but it sure wasn't any harder. I could not keep living like this. This man was turning into a psychotic monster, and I didn't have the strength nor the desire to make things right. The one thing I did want to continue was getting high. I knew I was on a destructive path, but the want and need to smoke crack outweighed everything else in my life, including my own children. I didn't care if I was homeless, or selling my body for a quick hit, it didn't matter to me. If I can run away and escape the reality for as long as I could, I would. This is what crack did for me. Crack took me from my worries. I didn't have to think about my fears, because once I took a hit, I feared nothing. I didn't have to worry about my feelings, because once I took a hit, I felt nothing. I was a Queen in my own eyes so during those moments I didn't care that I wasn't a Queen in anyone else's eyes. I turned numb to my failures, my hopes, worries and my horrible memories. I didn't care that my family wasn't looking for me. I was on my own in this world. My family means the world to me and now I look back at all these situations and wonder how my son copes from the trauma he felt in these situations. I wonder how my daughter feels now about her past when she was screaming and crying in the situations like above. How do they deal with their own pains? How do they fight the bad memories? My escape was crack. Hopefully their escape and coping mechanism is and was counseling and therapy. Most of us need therapy to deal with our past.

The next several months were the worst months of my life. I left Craig and hit the streets. I am so thankful that my daughter's dad took care of her. I didn't have to worry about her, I knew she was taken care of. My son was locked up in the boys' home, so I didn't have to worry about him either. It was just me, my little red station wagon and my drugs. Not often I would get hungry, but when I did, I would rummage through garbage cans to eat. I would sleep in my car and go days without showering. I honestly didn't think I deserved better. I would feel stuck when I was high, but the high would usually wear off in a few minutes and I would be stuck thinking about the guilt of not being a good mother. I loved my kids. I love them with all my heart, but they didn't think so. I mean, I don't blame them. Who would think their mom loved them if she wasn't there for them? Only drugs addicts would know how I felt, because they too understand addiction and how it can turn you against everything and everybody you know and love. I hated myself. I felt beaten and broken. I totally lost control of my entire life. I would ask myself; how did I get to this point? I realized my addiction had completely taken over, and crack cocaine helped me destroy my life.

The Power of the Present

I realized something about myself while I was battling life on the streets. I either was thinking about the past, or I was thinking about the future. Neither one of these stages were healthy for me. When I would think of my past, I would think all the way back to when I was a little kid experiencing rejection. Unfortunately, that pain was still fresh as if it was yesterday. I would think about how I have failed my kids, and I would play different scenarios over the years in my head where I failed. I would also think about the hands of my big cousins that would touch me when I didn't want to be touched.

Then, other times I would think about the future, and I was scared to move forward with a sober mind, and work through my issues. The hole I dug for myself was so deep, it was discouraging to think about overcoming it. I felt hopeless about tomorrow and how I would face my kids when I would see them. I was scared about facing anyone I knew from my past. They would probably look at me as a failure if I were to see them, so I tried to stay in the present. But the present was uncomfortable. I would use drugs to make myself numb to the moment. Let's talk about the present.

The present is our gift. We cannot do anything about the past, it is done and over with. We cannot do anything about the future, it is out of our control. But our present is our gift that we absolutely control to make the right decisions. But once we take our gift of the present for granted, misuse it and neglect it, we lose control of our future, and our present eventually turns into a regretful past. The more I used my present to get high, I neglected my future and fell victim to my past. My present moments would speed by quickly as I burned them, misused them, smoked them and downright wasted them. Our gift/present is the only time we have total control over, and when we use this time to use mood altering chemicals, we totally waste it. Then we become stuck thinking about our past and our futures, which feel like the gap in between the two grows more distant. We lose touch of reality and life appears to work against us. When I wasn't high, the present would really be difficult. I would try to commit suicide to alleviate the unbearable pain. I would jump out in front of cars in traffic. I would try and find drugs desperately to escape my gift. The present was just too much. It made me realize it was too hard to fight back. I'd rather just let my life go. My kids would be better off without me. The rest of my family wouldn't even care. I would think about my life and how I was driving Cadillacs and Lexus, wore lots of jewelry and flaunted my money, now to maneuvering through these ghetto streets in a station wagon trying to buy some crack cocaine so I can get out of the present. I didn't want my gift any longer. You can lead a horse to water, but you can't make him drink. Our present is worth pumping more uplifting thoughts into. I had been to several inpatient and outpatient drug treatments – a total of 12. The recovery mindset didn't stick with me, I wanted to get high to escape reality.

One of Many Encounters of God

The Road of Recovery

My last and final drug usage came from one night when I wanted to get high so badly. I went driving around in my beat-up red station wagon and I finally ended up parked outside my friend Sharon's house. I knew she would give me some money to get high. She always gave me money, so I knew this was a for sure trip. I knocked at her door, and she wouldn't unlock the door. I came to realize she wasn't home, so I went back to my car and thought about my next move. I was half drunk and was in a rage trying to figure out how I was going to get a fix. As I'm sitting in my car, a tall, middle aged white man comes and knocks at my window. I roll down my window enough for me to hear his crisp voice, and the guy asked if I was okay. I was not in the mood for this guy's crap. I was in a bad mood; my spirit was bad, and his energy was intrusive. I said no I'm not okay and please leave me alone. The guy then asked if he could pray for me. Pray for me?? "What is his deal?", I thought to myself, but I let him. He prayed for me and told me if I need anything to come up to the 3rd floor and he would let me lay down. He walks away from the car as I burst into tears. Now I'm crying and in a complete rage. I could not deal with this! I wanted to get high. Then another guy comes up and asks if he could pray for me. This guy was short, and middle aged as well. He had a hat on that said Jesus. I asked myself like what is going on with all these prayers. I told him yes, he could pray for me. He started to pray, and it took him awhile to finish. Once he finished, he walked away. Believe it or not, two minutes later, a third white man comes knocking on my window and asked to pray for me as well. By this time, I'm so irritated, I became loud and irate. He must have been with the first two guys because he says the exact same thing to me. He asks to pray for me. This was a bit hard to believe. I didn't understand why this was happening. I felt as if I was being the butt of a very unusual joke. Here I am trying to find some money to get high, and three random white men ask me if they could pray for me. How weird is that?

I fall asleep in the car, and I woke up the next morning. With the urge to still get high, I get out of the car and went to Sharon's apartment. I just knew she was home now and would be able to help me. Sharon answers the door and I walk right in.

"What's up JoJo, come on in girl".

"I'm cool", I said as I stepped into the house. "Girl, where were you at last night? I knocked and knocked. You weren't here? Your car was parked outside! Where were you? I needed a couple of dollars, and you were nowhere to be found!"

Sharon shot back, "I was here! Maybe I was sleep or something. I don't remember anyone knocking at this door baby. I didn't have any money last night anyway, I just now got some money from Otis." Otis was her man, and I didn't like him, and he didn't like me. But that is another story for another day. I turned to Sharon and quickly changed the subject; "Well it's all good now, I just gotta go up to the third floor to tell those guys thank you for praying for me last night. Girl, you have some nice neighbors."

"What are you talking about, JoJo this building doesn't have a third floor. And I don't have any nice neighbors!"

"Yes, you do, you have some neighbors that prayed for me last night. Three of them. They were all middle-aged white men too." At that moment, I looked up and realized there was no stairs going up to a third floor. What was going on? Was I going crazy?

Later in my journey, years later when I was talking to the Lord, he told me that those three guys were looking out for me, and he sent them to watch over me. They were the Father, Son and Holy Spirit. John 15:26 "When the Helper comes, whom I (Jesus) will send to you from the Father, that is the Spirit of truth who proceeds from the Father. He will testify about me…"

Anyway, Sharon gave me some money and I was out the door with the quickness. I was on a desperate search for some drugs to keep me from this awful reality I was stuck in. It hurt me to deal with the reality of my life and I had to get a blast of numbness so I could think. I can't remember how much I smoked in the next 72 hours of my life, but it was quite a bit. I also took some pills trying to overdose. I had no idea what the pills were, all I knew was I wanted to die sooner than later. During the next three to five days, I was on a hell ride. Self-destruction at its best! I hated me and who I stood for. I convinced myself I didn't want to be a parent anymore and I gave up on life, good thoughts and most of all, my daughter. At the time I was so broken, all I could think about was getting high, but when I was high, I hated being high. I know that sounds confusing, but when I would be high, I was very much conscious about my self-destructive decision. I hated myself for falling into the urges of this addiction. I would beat myself up about getting high, even when I was high. The world I once knew was gone, and I knew exactly why. The house with the white picket fence, my kids, my marriage, my friends, and more importantly my whole outlook on life was in shambles.

I knew I had to make a change, however getting the strength to do so is quite the challenge. I believe I hit rock bottom, and the biggest final blow came from my daughter. She told me she never wanted to speak to me again and she hung up on me. This was a 30 second phone call that ruined my little piece of strength I had left. Her voice burned my ears when she said it. I could hear the pain in her voice. She was so disappointed in me. I understood why. I hated myself. I tried to kill myself over and over. I would jump in front of speeding cars, or take handfuls of pills, but I never went anywhere. I would wake up feeling like a brand-new day has started. My mindset wouldn't allow me to take advantage of the day, but God would grant it to me anyway. After every attempt to end my life, either God jumped in and said, "it's not your time yet", or…well the more I think about this, that is it. There is no other explanation. God just wasn't ready for me to go. I believe He thought I had wronged so many, I must make amends somehow. So, after this last five-day episode of devastation, I was trying to climb out of the gutter. I reached out to family to help me, and no one would. I burned so many bridges, I realized I would have to do this on my own.

I made a call to Lutheran hospital and told them I was thinking about committing suicide. When I got there, I could barely talk. I needed a shower and a brush to tame my hair all over my head. If there was a picture of death in the dictionary, you would've seen me. But courage and desperation put me in front of the receptionist at Lutheran. She took one look at me and knew exactly where I needed to go. The hospital had a mental health ward to evaluate me. For the next three days, I laid in the bed barely moving. So many thoughts and so many tears. I swear I wanted to do better. I really did! I looked at everything I'd been through, and I wanted better. But how? How can I make it when my family and friends have turned against me? Not because of what they did, but because of the lies, the stealing, and the abuse I put myself through. I couldn't blame anyone for anything. This journey of self- diminishing hate came from somewhere, but I couldn't blame anyone besides myself. That was hard. I had to look in the mirror and face me.

But when my three days were up, they said they had to release me. I screamed, "I can't go back out there, I will die." I believe the nurse heard me throughout her entire being. She had compassion on me. She stared at me for a moment. I can tell she seen the pain in my eyes. She then said, "Let me see what I can do. "She left the room at a fast pace, looking determined. She came back into tell me there was a bed in Mecca and I could go there. So now I am going to Mecca – a treatment program for the 12th time. I gained a lot out of the program over the next few weeks. I met people that were in similar situations, trying to break through to see life differently. I realized I wasn't alone in this fight and there were people from all over with different backgrounds trying to get this monkey off their backs, as well. We would have group discussions, which I rarely talked out loud. I didn't have to. The ones that chose to speak spoke my life for me. I did a lot of listening, which made me humble enough to understand there were no differences between us. See, before I would think I was different, and nobody knew the struggles of my life. My emotions would cloud my feelings for other people. I always would think people were just out to hurt me, instead of thinking that hurt people are out here trying to cope.

One of the most monumental moments from treatment was when a counselor came in to talk with me. She was close to my age and had short gray hair. You can tell she had seen and heard it all because she had that look. When you work with recovering addicts for a while, you learn all the tricks and manipulative behaviors that come along with addiction. Many different walks of lives are impacted from drug usage, and this lady had seen it all. Her name was Paula. When she talked with me, I could tell she knew my story. She had seen me before in many different faces. She had seen the hurt and the pain, as if she was living it as well. One of the last times she spoke with me, she asked me, "JoJo, do you know who you are?" I immediately got defensive. Of course, I know who I am, what kind of question was that? I thought to myself why she would ask me that. Then it hit me. She asked me to take a few minutes in silence and think about who I am. I felt compelled by my lack of answers. I didn't know. I was a soul that was empty. I could tell you what I did or done. I could tell you what people have done to me, but I couldn't answer who I was. It's almost as if I wasn't living for me. I knew who JoJo was, but Mrs. JoAnna Davis was empty. Then after I looked at Paula, she looked into my eyes, and she knew that the answer was with me. She understood I couldn't articulate, but she knew I understood the question and how the question left me thinking. She then asked me to ask God who I was....

The Next Step

It was time to leave the treatment center after a few weeks, and I wasn't ready to go back to Des Moines. I owed a lot of drug dealers, and just left my name bad with several other people. I wasn't strong enough to face the repercussions of my bad ways. My exit interview went well. Paula helped me understand a few things I needed to do to move forward. First, Paula asked me what I was going to do. I didn't know. I said to Paula, "I just wish I was more like my grandmother because she knew how to let things roll off her and it didn't affect her. She never got stressed, and she loved the Lord." Paula looked up and said, "well that's not a hard task. You can learn to be like your grandmother." Up until that moment, I felt it wasn't that easy, I believed. I believed I was beneath damn near everyone and everything. A lightbulb went off instantly. I asked her if she really thought I could be like my grandmother, and she then said, "it would be easy for you to be like her. Hang out with people that acted and thought like your grandma. They are all around, you must change your playground and playmates." My life changed instantly. Psalm 30: 5 "Weeping may endure for a night, but a joy comes in the morning". I realized this was the thing to do. I gotta go to church!

So, our lives are full of trials and tribulations. We go through so many things in life. We struggle with our thoughts, our surroundings, our misguided paths, ALL to wake up one day and understand from this moment forward. What a moment this was! All my years of addiction, stemming from all the years of rejection, abuse and hatred. All these years of learning to come to this present gift of a moment. Right now! You mean, I had to go through all of that to get here?? It appears God took me through a journey of turbulence and turmoil, so he could bring me to right now. I think it could have been a lot easier if He just would have told me and I listened. LOL. But what do I know? At that moment, I realized I had to walk my journey through. I came too far to give up, and "coming too far" was a part of my purpose. God had to take me through some battles. All the battles to bring me right here talking to Paula. The lady that knew exactly what to say to me to get me moving in the right direction. God is real.

So, I wasn't ready to go be a part of the free world yet. I was very vulnerable and urges to get high were frequent. I went to a long-term treatment facility, and in this place, you had to get a job. They would give us tokens to catch the bus right outside and go to wherever you needed to go. This could make or break a recovering addict because you are around triggers and life tempts you to take the wrong direction. The facility doesn't hold your hand through this, and they give you enough rope to hang yourself. It is very easy to fall into the devil's playground and end up back at square one. I was scared. I owed a lot of people money. I also didn't want to see certain areas, as it might trigger me to use. Funny, because God was talking to me more during this time period. Maybe He wasn't talking to me more, maybe I was just listening more and handing Him my life to guide me. It's called getting out of the way. Anyway, He told me, "JoAnna, I will blind the sight of your enemies". Right then, I made a choice to believe, and move forward. I got dressed in the full intention on going out into the world to seek employment. I took a token and walked to the bus stop right around the corner. I breathed the fresh air. I felt rejuvenated and alive. Over on 6th Ave was a plasma center where you could donate plasma and they would pay you. I needed to start there. I would put a little bit of money in my pocket, and instead of smoking it all up, I would save and plant some seeds. Across the parking lot from this plasma center was a convenience store where all the neighborhood regulars would use. Some would hang out right outside of the building and sell drugs, fight or panhandle their way through life.

After I donated plasma, I took my money over to the store to buy something to drink and there stood one of my old dealers. I didn't panic on the outside, but I was trembling on the inside. I didn't know what he was going to do. He came up to me smiling, with a mouth full of gold teeth. "JoJo, what's good baby? Hey. You are looking good. I see you! You know that money you owe me, don't worry about it. Take care of yourself. I mean that." He looked at me and I could tell he was serious. He continued to talk to me. "This ain't for you. Let these folks have this out here (he pointed all around the street we were on) because you are different."

"Yeah, I'm different." That night I was back at the center and was unwinding and reflecting on this day. I still was trying to process my old drug dealer letting me go unscathed. It was so unlikely of him because I owed quite a bit to him. For him to turn and say no worries was so different. I just so happened to open to the book Psalms, and it clearly stated. The first line my eyes fell on said Psalms 64:2 "God will hide you from your enemies, hide me from the secret counsel of the wicked, from the insurrection of the workers of iniquity." I swear God pops up everywhere.

So, I got a job! I was a manager at a clothing store! I enjoyed working because I felt like I was helping other people. I felt like I was an example of triumph, even if you didn't know me, you would one day.

My daughter was doing well with her dad. I am truly blessed to have a great father to my daughter. I will never know how much pain I've caused her, but at least she had some balance. I love her with all my heart, and once she said she would never speak to me again, we have worked through that. There are still light years ahead to restore or replenish our relationship, but I'm here for it all. We started to talk more and that helped me out a lot.

At night, I was learning the Bible through teaching other women at the facility. It was a blessing because this was the first time, I was reading the Bible and applying the scriptures to my own life. It was also a blessing because these women were looking up to me to show them the way. A lot were younger, and a few were older. They looked up to me to guide them. That added responsibility was what I needed so I could keep myself on my square. I needed to feel that they depended on me and my righteous actions nowadays. I wasn't strong enough to do it on my own yet. A few of the managing ladies at the facility didn't like that I was having Bible groups in the evening. They thought I was trying to be the boss, but I truly wasn't. I was taking a backseat and letting my humbleness guide me because once in my life, I felt that I was being guided the right way, and I was open to the spirit of God and His teachings. They felt like I was being a showoff and coming off like I was creating a cult following.

One of the managers even said to me that I was "trying to be the leader and we just can't have that!" I started to feel as if the staff started picking on me. They would write me up and give me warnings for the most senseless things. I recall one of those senseless times being when I came in ten minutes late from work. Judy, (the nighttime admin), came knocking at my door and told me we needed to talk. As I welcomed her in, she had a paper and a pen in her hand. She turns to me with a stern look "You have been insubordinate, and we need you to sign this. This states you have acknowledged once again all the rules set forth in this facility and any other infraction will result in you being put on level one." Being out on level one would mean that I lose privileges, like phone use and leisure time with the other ladies. It would also mean that I would be one step closer to Level 2 which is a denial of completion of the program and asked to leave. I refused to sign the document. Why did I need to sign this knowing they are trying to alienate me from my peers? They just want me to be isolated from everyone. It didn't seem like they were concerned about me being in recovery, they just didn't want me to have influence on the other women for some reason.

Since I didn't sign the paper, I was put on level one. That was the best thing they could do for me. It felt like my time there was coming to an end anyway. As Judy was leaving my room, I slammed the door behind her and sat down on my bed to think my next move through. I asked God for guidance, and he told me to look for a place and this is what I was determined to do.

The next day, I started looking for places to live. It didn't take me long to find it, since I was so determined to get out of the facility. I didn't have much money, but a check for $188.00. I found a place that didn't have a lot of space. It was an efficiency. It has roaches and mice, but hey it was a place. I went back to the facility and was asked to sign the behavioral contract. I refused so they said I had 24 hours to vacate. The next morning the apartment manager called me while I was at work and asked if I was still interested in the apartment. I said YES, but I only have a check for $188.00. He said that's ok come sign your lease and get the keys. I was very grateful to have my own furnished place. I couldn't wait to return to the facility that evening and pack my stuff and get the heck out of there. As I was packing, Judy approached me asking if I changed my mind and wanted to sign the paper to acknowledge the rules of the facility. I was so excited to tell her to jump off a cliff, but I told her kindly, "Judy, I've actually found a place of my own and I will be leaving here tonight." As I packed a few of the last essentials I had into my bag, Judy says, "well what are you going to do?" She said this in a way of sarcasm, and I could feel the bad energy steaming off her clothes. I looked at her and told her, "I'm going to live my life under the supervision and guidance of my Lord." At that moment, I grabbed my few belongings and started to move around Judy to the exit. The door never seemed so bright. "Well good luck", Judy says. I didn't have time to feed into her comment to examine if it was sincere or just a sarcastic remark.

Over the last several years, I've been in and out of treatment facilities well over 12 times. I've been down this road before, and this felt different. I felt this was the last time! I now had a life to go live, and it was time I put myself first and get out of the way that God has paved for me. It was time for me to take guidance and surrender my voice of answers, and to allow my voice of questions to take over. I needed to start this fight, and it felt so good.

I unlocked the door with my keys to my little efficiency, and as I turned the light on, I saw my little kitchen rigged with a few older appliances. Immediately to the left of the kitchen area, was a rollout mattress that was just covered with a white sheet. As I look down at the stain-embedded carpet, all I can do was smile. Yes, I was flat broke! Yes, I had these four walls of simplicity, but I felt full. I felt my world was changing for the better, and I was so ready to embrace my changes. I looked at my place as a home, because I've seen so much worse than this. I've slept in crack houses with strangers getting high, and a stench that reeked of death. I've slept in houses that were full of family and felt distant and alone. But this was mine. It was a start. But it was an end to a life of destruction.

I couldn't wait to call my baby girl and tell her we have a place. Even though she told me she was never going to talk to me again. I dialed her number as I sat on my bed with tears in my eyes. She answered after four rings. I hurried and blurted out what I was dying to tell her. "I know you are mad at me...but I got a place for us. It's not much. It's really small, but it's ours." Surprisingly, without any hesitation, my daughter said, "ok mommy." That is all I needed to hear. She is giving me another chance! She is allowing me to be a part of her life and God knows that is all I wanted in life is to be a part of my children's lives. I loved my kids. I couldn't wait to start showing and proving to my daughter that she was my world.

The next few weeks were a great transition. It was challenging, but very rewarding. My daughter and I were growing closer again. I didn't have a car, but I was getting there. The neighborhood we were in was not a bad area. It had a few moments here and there, and drugs were plentiful, but for the most part, it was quiet. The area showed signs of hope. It had a corner store and a laundry mat. People were coming and going and didn't have time to meddle in other's affairs. It wasn't a place of misery. God was showing me where I needed to be, how I needed to move and what I needed to do. One day as I walked down a few blocks over to the bus stop, I witnessed a few drug dealers doing what they do, and God spoke to me and said, Romans 12:2 "do not conform to the patterns of this world but be transformed by the renewing of your mind, that you may prove what is that good and acceptable and perfect will of God." That said it all to me. I had to have tunnel vision and carry out my duties as a servant of Christ and a provider for my babies. The next morning, God told me to open the Bible every day and read, so I took a moment and opened it and started reading. I opened it right to the verse above. How incredible is this? I see on paper what he said to me yesterday. God is so real. I see God every day because I opened and allowed myself to receive. Now every day I wake up, I take a few breaths and then I utter the words from Psalms 23, "the Lord is my shepherd, I shall not want".

I engulfed myself into church the next several weeks. I started to love this routine, and I loved my daughter being here through it all. Do you know how proud I would be when I would walk into church with my daughter? Everything seemed to be falling right in line. I was becoming a true servant of the Lord. I grew as an evangelical spirit and would enlighten anyone that crossed my path with His words and His name. I started to grow and become respected in the church as well. At this time, I envisioned a lot of different activities and events that I could coordinate. I started looking at putting pieces together like Legos. God was showing me how to move and create. He also told me to put together a Gospel Explosion event that I started to work towards.

The Last Relapse

You must check yourself and always stay in control of your moves. You cannot control anyone else in this world besides yourself, and how you react. Discipline is tough at times. When you are an addict, there is no such thing as a cure. You don't just wake up one day and become fixed from your addiction. Some of us are led to believe that we have little to no power over our addiction, and this is even taught in Narcotics Anonymous. When you have created an addiction, it is a never-ending battle every single day to stay clean. You must watch your playmates. Your close friends and acquaintances can put you in situations where you will be tested, and depending on how strong you are, you might fall short. We can also get cocky with our recovery. Especially if we have a few great days under our belt, and we start to accumulate a decent way of life. I had my own place and started to see great things in my future. I would work every day and kept to a decent routine. Next thing I know, like time and time before, I'm sitting in a crack house full of dope fiends smoking dope all night. It happens just like that. If you hang in the same playgrounds with the same playmates, expect the same results at some point. I had a man take me out on a date, and I know he was using, but I still went. We went to dinner, and after we left, we stopped by an old friend's house. We walked into the house, and I saw several of my old smoking buddies and guess what? All of them were smoking. I bet you can guess that it didn't take me long to fall right in and get to smoking with them. That was a horrible experience I went through, but it was needed for me to take that next step. So here I am, smoking dope and getting high with the same folks and it hit me. I concluded that this is not fun anymore. I concluded that I didn't need this anymore. Before you know it, it's 6am. I was surrounded by suffering people just like me, that wanted a way out but couldn't shake the monkey off their backs. Until this moment, I was unclear of my path in life. I was slowly getting things together in my mind to tackle life, but just didn't fully know the steps. I wanted to help people learn God, and how he was helping me change in my life. But I wasn't sure my steps. Until this moment, at 6am, sitting around a room full of hopelessness, sadness and despair, I decided to make a change, and to stand on that change. I decided that drugs were just not for me anymore. I decided to fully commit to the Lord, and to serve him. I looked around at everyone in that living room and realized my purpose was to help people get out of these situations right here! These situations that these rooms create are crippling for addicts. Just imagine being in a room full of addicts that would use and use inflicting self-destruction.

Once your high wears off, you have landed from cloud 9 and you are back to reality. You are back to the reality that you were using to escape from, and it hurts. This is when the sadness sets in, as well as the guilt. The guilt for falling for our habits and neglecting everyone and everything to get our fix. The sadness from being rejected in the world and facing the reality that you are back on the ground and can't run anymore, until the next flight. Enough is enough! I had enough! It was time to walk away from this and as I rose to my feet to walk towards the door, I felt the weight of the world lift from my shoulders. I felt lighter on my feet, with the baggage behind me. As I was leaving the house, I said my farewells to each one that crossed my path on my way to the car. I knew I was changing, and my life would never be the same. I got in my car and looked in my rear-view mirror one last time. I saw the rugged road I've always traveled. I shook my head, cranked my car up and drove off towards the sun. It was bright, and so was this new path that was paced out right in front of me.

The Sun

Ever since I started being an evangelist, I had a great church home. I loved the pastor and First Lady. They both used to inspire and persuade me to go further with the Lord, and lead people. They knew the path I was on and supported me. After my last relapse the night before, I left the crack house I was right in time for me to get ready for church. I never wanted to go to church so bad in my life. I hurried home, showered and dressed and walked into church a few minutes early. It was a great time. The sermon was on point, to where I thought he was talking directly to me. As the music started to play, God told me to "dance till it rains". I didn't know exactly what that meant at the time, but I started to feel the spirit move me. I was loving the vibes and really felt like I was being healed from everything. I started dancing and sweating and yelling. I was feeling this moment all too well. My pastor yelled out to the congregation, "it's never too late to turn around!" At this moment, I asked God for forgiveness for my relapse. I knew at that moment I would never touch that poison again. Drenched from the tears and sweat, I noticed I felt like I was in the rain. This had to be what God meant when he said, "dance till it rains". I was soaking wet and felt so clean and revamped. That day forward, I jumped into doing a lot of street ministry.

The duties of an evangelist are broad. We travel all over the lands trying to touch lost souls and give direction. I love my work, and I genuinely love to see other's catch what I caught in the word of Christ. Once you feel the magnitude of God, it changes you and makes you want to share what you feel with the world. Some are receptive, and some grow to have understanding over time. The more people I started to touch, the more I felt that I needed to create my own congregation. The more I could hear and feel God calling me to build a ministry. I knew I had a greater purpose than what I was doing then. I was under the influence of my pastor and First Lady. Pastor always encouraged me to do more. He told me I had great purpose in this field, and I was ready to make things happen on a bigger level. A lot of my bigger thoughts were propelled by the encouragement my pastor would give me. I learned a lot under his leadership, but I felt when it was time to spread my wings and get the acceptance from him to do so, I was rejected. I submitted a proposal for a program I wanted to implement, and I feel I was brushed off and not taken seriously.

However, the program I wanted to implement was used and the name was changed. The rejection I felt was huge, and it reminded me of all the times of my past where I was rejected by people I trusted. But the difference between now and then is now I have a relationship with my Lord and Savior, Jesus Christ. He is showing me how to handle things by leading me. I guess He has always tried to lead, but now I choose to listen. So, I picked up the pieces of my rejected soul, and I put them back together outside of the church. I left! I'm doing my last time at this church, during the service, I heard the song "dance the way that David danced", and I heard a voice say in my ear, "shake the dust from your feet and never look back." Matthew 10:14 "And whoever will not receive you nor hear your words, when you depart from that house or city, shake off the dust from your feet." Well, that's what I did. I danced my way out of the church and from that day forward, I pressed on without and started my own journey to help people who were willing to help themselves find the Lord.

I spent the next year or so going from church to church, studying pastors and learning how to fulfill my purpose of evangelism. I was learning what to do and more importantly, what not to do. I learned so much from so many different pastors. I stayed focused on the mission and stayed praying for my sobriety. I also prayed for the strength to keep standing in this purpose regardless of how challenging it become. When you start to listen to God and understand how to submit to his lead, things start happening around you that make it easy for you to walk right into the righteous path of your purpose. Your eyes and ears will be open to receive the direction because you will be paying attention to all the signs.

One sign I paid attention to was back in 2012, when God told me I need to buy a building in small town Iowa. A few days later, I was in a conversation with a great local pastor that told me the same thing, He said, "God spoke to me for the last three days and he told me you will buy a building in Southwestern Iowa. Creston, Iowa to be exact. This was enough to make me wake up and start looking. It just so happened at this time of my life I was really engulfed in the book of Ezekiel chapter two. For those that are not familiar, Ezekiel was a prophet that God called to go to the children of Israel, a rebellious nation that had rebelled against God. Ezekiel 2: 1-5 "And He said to me "son of man, stand on your feet, and I will speak to you". 2. Then the Spirit entered me when He spoke to me and set me on my feet, and I heard Him who spoke to me. 3. And He said to me, "son of man, I am sending you to the children of Israel, to a rebellious nation that has rebelled against Me; they and their fathers have transgressed against Me to this vary day. 4. For they are (a)impudent and stubborn children. I am sending you to them, and you shall say to them, "thus says the Lord God As for them, whether they hear or whether they refuse they are a rebellious house – yet they will know that a prophet has been among them." His task wasn't easy, but I knew this was my calling and I had to take heed to the difficulties Ezekiel endured. He was determined to spread the word regardless of what he went through.

It was a bright and early morning when I put the Bible down on my nightstand, face down opened to the page I left. I got up that moment, brushed my teeth and got dressed. I drove 75 miles to Creston, Iowa very optimistic that I would find something. I reached Creston and I immediately thought this place was vacant. I didn't see a lot of life. The population wasn't quite 5,000 people, so in some areas it looked deserted. Creston is approximately a five-mile radius of a few dilapidated houses, fields of corn, a community college and a university. I turned onto a gravel road and saw a building that was a decent size. It sat right on the corner. I could tell this building was vacant. It didn't have a sign or anything, but I was determined to find out more information about this building. I looked across the street and noticed a corner store. A strange looking man was there. I heard God's voice say go ask if he knows who owns the building. So, I walked to the store. I pushed open the door to the store and there was a blond hair, blue eye lady sitting on the far end of a counter. "Excuse me ma'am, do you know what is going on with that building across the street? I would like to inquire about owning it." I pointed towards the direction of the building. She says "well I do. I'm a real estate agent and I have a listing down the street which is a church." My mouth dropped. This is how God works. I drove quickly over to the church and met the real estate lady there. I asked her if the owner would be willing to lease the church to me. She explained to me that he wanted to sell it and she didn't think he would lease. She called him and he agreed to meet me there on Friday. The church looked perfect. I went home ecstatic about what I found and couldn't wait to meet him a couple days later.

That Friday, I gassed up my car on a mission back to Creston to talk to the owner of the church. I only had $500 on me. That was all the money I had. That money was supposed to pay my own mortgage back home, but I was willing to take a chance and see what I could do to make this happen. This is how strong God's word was to me. He told me about this, and I followed and found! I got to the building and parked and there was an older gentleman with a few strands of hair on his head standing in the front of the building. I looked at the building and almost started to cry. It was beautiful, small and said JoAnna all over it. The little building was covered with older white paint. It was a country style church for sure. When I entered, I immediately saw the original old wood pews. It reminded me of "The Little House on the Prairie". Like the old country movies, it was about 5 pews on each side. It had been sitting for about three years and no one had been using it. It smelled empty and a little cold, but when I walked in, I immediately knew that God had called me to that building. It was perfect! The owner, Jim was standing there looking at me light up as I walked down the aisles, smiling. Anyone could see that I was excited. I had tears of joy and I haven't even started the negotiations yet for this. It's not even mine yet, but I felt in my spirit that it would be.

Jim and I were making small talk for a little bit and then he asks me, "Joanna, do you pray a lot?" I answered, "yes, I do. All the time!" He then says, "Well I don't pray, but I pretty much own most of Creston, Iowa." We worked out some details with some minor expenses and he told me he wanted me to have it. This wise older man was very kind and generous. He says he's been hoping someone would turn it into a nice church because the town needs one.

A month later, I, Joanna Davis was holding a meet and greet in the town of Creston Iowa for my new church! I didn't even have to advertise! The presence of God was all over this. When I set the date for the meet and greet, somehow the local newspaper caught wind and that's all she wrote! I didn't need to spend any money at all. I also got a call from a local resident, John, asking if I needed a sound person and that he would love to come help me. From that day God had given me my first 7 members of the church which included John, his wife, his 3 children and a friend. Can you believe, in a small country town where I didn't know not one person, I was opening a church? To this day, I'm still in shock that God took me here and took care of me through the whole process. The meet and greet was a success with over 125 people showing up. One of those people was the mayor! He was excited that we were making this happen. Opening Sunday, I was scrambling all over to find a sound system. My good friend who is a DJ back home in Des Moines helped me with a few speakers. Everything was working out. When I opened the doors to the church that first Sunday morning, I had a full house – the church seats approximately 50. I was beyond proud, and nervous. I was also anxious to start my journey, and we all made it a great time. It was so great; the size of my church doubled the next week. Before you knew it, the city of

Creston was being enlightened and empowered by God, and I was the messenger receiving great energy from my congregation.

I consistently drove every Sunday for a few months, and then relocated in a home right behind the church. But I didn't stop with just service on Sundays. We created huge revivals, and the city was very receptive to doing more and more with my church. We also started a restaurant and a thrift store called "Neighbors Loving Neighbors". It was a great five years in Creston, and I visit regularly now to see the growth of the city and to remind myself where I started on my journey. It felt so good to be a part of helping provide miracles for people. There were some people that really needed the word of God and I'm so thankful for being able to help them.

Looking at my congregation motivated me. I guess, when you are living your purpose, your purpose keeps you out of harm's way. I no longer have the desire to do drugs. I no longer felt the need to dwell on my last rejections. I felt that the chapter of my life that was dark, was over! My stresses that came along with everyday life seemed to be manageable. I turned to working for the Lord to help me through and by doing so, I was and can help so many others.

Oh, and I found love again!

In 2015, I ran into a childhood boyfriend. I think God said to me, "you put three solid years into laying the groundwork for miracles for others, let's reward you with a husband." I remember seeing Charles for the first time in years, on Facebook and it was like instant love all over again. After that we exchanged numbers and started dating. It was an incredible feeling. I was serving a great purpose in life. I was growing by the day and here comes this man that just so happened to be growing in the right direction as well. We got married after three months of dating. We knew it was real. He understood me. He comforted me and was every bit of the man I prayed for having one day. We laughed and joked about everything. It was just so natural to be with him. I was completely myself, no changing who I am to fit into his world. It just fell perfectly together.

A few of the people that were in my circle disagreed with us being married so quickly. Charles was in and out of prison, so I understood how it would look to some people, but I didn't care. Charles has a wonderful heart and he made me feel good. We were so much alike in ways that mattered. We got along great. I honestly believe God made Charles for me and he made me for Charles.

Keeping family ties can be a downfall for some people. Some of us are not able to grow because we allow ourselves to stay "solid" with certain family members that do not mean us any good. I believe Charles had a lot of issues trying to grow with me, but at the same time stay loyal to family members that he felt he owed. We would talk about how his family being over all the time was an issue. They would all gather and drink and sometimes get into silly arguments. Steven was second oldest brother, and he had a drinking problem, so a lot of the times when Charles and he got together, it was short lived. I felt as if Charles hung out with his family because he didn't want to venture out and meet new people. He was very comfortable where he was at, and that makes it easy to fall into unhealthy situations. For a lot of us, some of our family members are toxic. However, we have a sense of obligation to hold with them so we at times cater to those members that have negative energy.

One thing I have learned in my life journey is that you must do what's right for you. You will never be anything to anybody if you don't have a sound mind. In order to bring yourself to a level of growth that is needed to be happy, you must love from a distance at times. No matter who it is, mother, father, brother, sister, friend…if the chemistry and energy isn't uplifting, you will not be able to elevate. This doesn't mean you love any less, you just love from a distance.

Everything was great until he started drinking more and hanging out with family. He had 2 brothers. His younger brother Dale was so disrespectful and always was instigating and causing problems. They spent a lot of time going back and forth about irrelevant topics, but they were passionate about their opinions. Charles would always say, "give him a pass, he's immature." Charles would always ignore Dale because Dale would always try to be the center of attention.

Also, I'm not judging or knocking anyone who drinks alcohol with the later statements, but I've found out along my journey that when alcohol is present, there is no telling what can happen. Alcohol is a huge influencer, and everyone is at different levels with handling the toxic chemicals. Some can handle drinking, some can't. I have chosen to not deal at all with it because I've never had anything good or productive from my consumption and alcohol was trauma for me because of my experiences with my father as a child.

A couple years went by, and I am having the time of my life for several reasons. I finally feel happy. I am doing what I love, and that is spreading the word. My congregation is growing! I have a wonderful husband. My daughter and I are growing closer, and I am drug free. I am thinking clearly. What a peace of mind it is to be able to think about the present and think about the future in a positive way.

My forward thinking was starting to give me life and an enormous amount of energy that I never felt before. I was no longer thinking about how miserable I was. I was no longer thinking about how I was a failure. My thoughts were busy thinking about creating my next move. I became accustomed to grabbing life and making things happen, instead of waiting on the perfect timing, or the perfect energy. God allowed me to create my own energy and my energy started to carry me. I was able to see my potential and purpose – my Devine calling.

God also led me to a path that created so much production and creativity. I loved being able to reach people through Him. Everywhere I went, there was always an opportunity to shed light, understand, or learn about the Lord. When we focus on Him, we are shown the value in Him from what we experience. A lot of times, we don't contribute our everyday moves to God. We only call upon him when we need guidance, or something materialistic. Or we call on him when we made a great move in life, and we are being rewarded. However, what about the moves in between that shape and mold us for the result of success? All the struggles and bad choices that we learned from are just as important as the outcome. The outcome of triumph would never come without the troubles before.

Today, I can appreciate the moments of my life that weren't so good, and quite challenging at the time. I am so happy that I took the route of trusting God to lead. I sat down and got out of my own way.

After all the bad parenting decisions, drug addictions, God still had a plan for me. After not putting myself first for years, and treating my own life as a practice run, God didn't throw me away. God was still here to protect me. My story goes to show you that life happens every day. Regardless of what happens, it's not too late to turn it around.

Fast forward to 2017, where my life has grown into the routine of normalcy. My name is starting to ring in churches all over the United States and internationally. I'm living my purpose and being rewarded daily. Of course, struggles come and go, but handling business through it all is so much easier when we are sober and living the will of God for our lives. We can fight and see clearly. On the morning of August 4th, 2017, I woke up in the middle of the night and I used the restroom, and I looked up and there was a silhouette of a grim reaper. I couldn't see a face, but I heard a sound. The grim reaper said, "I'm coming to take him out". I get back in the bed and tell Charles. He said "Joanna, you're just tired, you need to go to bed!" Oh, my poor husband. Here he is trying to walk his righteous walk and his wife is always feeling something and saying something crazy. He must think I'm so crazy from hearing me always speaking from my gifts. So I go back to bed, and when we get up, Charles is getting ready for work.

I was excited for a women's retreat that I was helping facilitate in Afton, Iowa. This was a weekend adventure with a bunch of great ladies in the ministry. As I was preparing to leave for the weekend, I was talking to Charles as he was leaving out for work. He kissed me on the forehead, and he walked out of the door. I didn't think anything of it. It was a typical day. Later in the afternoon, I called him while he was at work. He tells me he was about to get off work and he says he was about to mow the lawn and feed the dog. He said his brother was going to come over and they were going to exchange some weight equipment. I told him not to have any partying going on in the house because I knew his family was going to be in town and they always liked to be together. He said he would not have a party and he was just going to hang out and take it easy.

August 5th, 2017, at 4am changed my life forever! This was truly a demonic attack and heavily spiritual warfare on my life and my husband. I will go further in detail in future publications, so stay tuned. Anyway, that morning, I was woken up by a phone call telling me I need to come home. I thought this was so ironic. Charles gave the phone to his sister-in-law, and she says, "they're up to their same old shit! They are fighting as usual, and Charles cut Dale and he's bleeding. You need to come home. I gotta go and check on Dale again." So, I quickly packed my bag and drove home. On my way home, I felt something was devastatingly wrong. I hit the corner to my house, and I see yellow tape. My house was blocked off and was a real-life crime scene! My husband was gone and in jail. I just collapsed in the middle of the street. Charles was in jail being charged with first degree murder, and my brother-in-law, was dead. They had started to fight, and my husband was charged with murdering his own brother. My life has changed forever. Just when I thought things were nearing perfect, my life mate is gone!

And the rumors started flying. I heard everything from it was a drug deal gone wrong, to it was a set up. People would just make up anything to press a conversation, and it wouldn't even matter if it was real or fake news. But rumors can be bad. They can cause an impact on things, and it was really a bad impact on my ministry. People started leaving the church and it was hard to keep that going on top of losing the love of my life abruptly. It was a lot of stress caused by this. Anytime your life goes from two incomes to one, it gets rough. But the biggest part, I felt like I lost my best friend. I felt like my soulmate was just taken away. Is this what the grim reaper meant by when he said he was coming to take him out? Who knows, but I believe so.

As Charles sat in jail, I'm on the outside trying to pick up the pieces from my broken household and my broken ministry. After trying to work it out in the small town where my church was, I decided to move my ministry to Des Moines. I didn't have much to move, since my congregation dwindled too nearly no one. Some members would travel to Des Moines. My work here started to be productive, and my ministry was starting to flourish here in Des Moines. As I would talk to Charles on the phone, he would encourage me to keep going. He was like my biggest motivator during this time period. He gave me the motivation to stand up to the naysayers and keep building what was meant to be. I would cry myself to sleep at night. I would feel pressures and stresses that I never felt before. My church here then started thriving.

In 2019, Charles ended up getting a sentence of 50 years, 35 years mandatory. I was devastated. Talk about being heartbroken. I believed I was going to spend the rest of my life with this man. We talked every day, and even being in jail, he was my best friend. Life throws you curves all the time. I believe when we aren't strong enough to push our own selves through the storm, God gives you someone to strengthen you. I'm sure a lot of parents can agree that they wouldn't be where they are today if they didn't have to take care of someone else.

Well, during all this pain and suffering, I found out I had a grandson. I went through all the paperwork to adopt him, and here I am taking care of a little boy. My precious little grandson, Joshua has given me a whole new purpose. Not only has he given me purpose, but he has also given me a chance to be strong for him. He depends on me. My daily life routine has changed dramatically because I have a responsibility that I wouldn't change for the world. He has given me a sense of direction!

During this time recently I have started a women's transitional housing center called Foundational Stones International. My church is growing by the day, and I am smiling daily. I have also done international preaching in

Africa, Guatemala, Mexico and Trinidad. Life isn't perfect, but I'm finally giving myself a chance that I needed. A chance to trust myself and grow. We all have the days where we want to throw in the towel. Our lives seem unmanageable and so hard to compete. However, we must realize we aren't competing with anyone. Our world and our journey are our test which becomes our testimony to share with others. We live life with a purpose of being better than who we were yesterday. What we learned yesterday gives us hope today. We are God's children, and we make our world the way we need it to be when we get out of our way and try ourselves. Give yourself a chance in this world.

Today, I am happy, and I am free. Am I free from pain? No, not at all. But I can deal with my pains today knowing that the joy of the Lord is my strength and where I'm weak He is made strong. Nehemiah 8: 10 (KJV) "for the joy of the LORD is your strength." 2 Corinthians 12:9-10 New King James Version 9 And He said to me, "My grace is sufficient for you, for the strength is made perfect in weakness. Therefore, most gladly I will rather boast in my infirmities, that the power of Christ may rest upon me. 10 Therefore I take pleasure in the infirmities, in reproaches, in needs, in persecution in distresses, for Christ's sake. For when I am weak, then I am strong." What we focus on matters. How we look at things matters. How we form our opinion of ourselves matters to how we tackle the world. Your strength is in you, the hope of Glory, Christ Jesus! 1 John 4:4 NKJV 4 "You are of God, little children, and have overcome then because He who is in you is greater than He who is in the world." You must just keep digging. Dig through the layers of hurt and guilt. Dig through the hate and the self-doubt. We all have regrets. Some would say I regret, but I say I have no regrets. Why? Because all that I have been through has shaped who I am. We all have moments that fill the day. If I know that I'm living in the moment, I can make sure I don't have a bad day. But those bad moments come, but they won't disrupt my purpose, and always giving God the Glory!

I love my kids! I wish I would have been there more for them when I was younger and weaker. I'm here now. No, I don't have tons of college degrees and academic awards, but I do have accolades and tremendous accomplishments. No, I don't have all the money in the world, but I am able to think things through and generate an income to support me and my grandson. I have a rough past, but who doesn't? My future is what I choose to make it along with the assistance from God. It's in us, not on us. As I continue this life journey, I want to encourage everyone to stay the course and to forgive yourself. Love yourself. Train yourself to be good to you, even when it's hard. We owe it to ourselves to give the best to us and our surroundings. I want to continue my life. There was a time I didn't want to continue my life. There was a time when my mind focused on the dark. I love you all and I love the sun. Let's all shine together by digging up the dark that we have stored within. The pain can be altered to power. Our pain is energy. Energy never is destroyed, but it can be transferred. Use pain to focus on the power it creates. Proverbs 3:5-6 5" Trust in the Lord with all your heart and lean not on your own understanding: 6 In all your ways acknowledge Him and He shall (a) direct your paths." I love you all, and I love me!

Sometimes we love
And our hearts are broken
We dream
And our hopes are shattered
We wish
And our desires are unfulfilled
We give freely
And are left empty-handed
And we care for others
And aren't loved in return
And those who we once most admired and valued
Do not reciprocate our affection.
Sometimes we undergo a process of loss and heartbreak
And are left feeling broken
And lacking hope
As we fail to realise
That we are not destined to remain stuck in this cycle indefinitely
And that in life
What lets go of you
Leads you home
What rejects you
Empowers you to embrace yourself fully
And that someone's lack of love for you
Is ultimately a reflection of them rather than you.

~ Tahlia Hunter

THIS IS THE DAY THE LORD HAS

LCL

www.ingramcontent.com/pod-product-compliance
Ingram Content Group UK Ltd.
Pitfield, Milton Keynes, MK11 3LW, UK
UKHW020134250726
13967UKWH00002B/656

9 781387 656158